ALL CREATION: GOD'S GLORY

A Workbook Inviting One to Appreciate Everything in the Universe

Rev. Leo McIlrath, DMin

ALL CREATION: GOD'S GLORY
A WORKBOOK INVITING ONE TO APPRECIATE EVERYTHING IN THE UNIVERSE

Author Credits: Leo McIlrath

iUniverse books may be ordered through booksellers or by contacting:

iUniverse
1663 Liberty Drive
Bloomington, IN 47403
www.iuniverse.com
1-800-Authors (1-800-288-4677)

ISBN: 978-1-5320-2184-8 (sc)
ISBN: 978-1-5320-2185-5 (e)

"The cover is emblazoned with a colorful spiral, manifesting the diversity of all created beings (humans, animals, vegetation and non living entities,) In its midst, and at it very core, our God (YHWH), who, "in the beginning," created the seeds of all that ever existed and will come to be, allowing for all to evolve into our ever-expanding universe."

Print information available on the last page.

iUniverse rev. date: 05/03/2017

INTRODUCTION

Several years ago, while serving as director of the Department of Elderly Services/ City of Danbury, in Connecticut, I was continuously faced with a question that perplexed a number of senior citizens:

- *"Am I losing my mind? I can't remember anything these days."*
- *"I often lock the keys in the car; I leave the lights on all night long;"*
- *"I go shopping and only bring home a few of the items I had hoped to purchase"*
- *"I miss several meetings!"*
  For many of those concerned, the problem wasn't all that serious. They were simply unfocused, while handling very busy calendars.

However, real or not, the concern about memory loss, often exacerbated the stress, leaving people in various states of anxiety. Sound familiar? It certainly does to me! Choosing to address this issue head-on, I scheduled the first of many classes at our local senior center on memory techniques. Utilizing several well-proven procedures, such as mnemonics, picturing, pegging, the use of our alphabet's letters, acronyms, etc., we worked with the participants in a fun-filled and non-threatening manner. One activity that grew out of these sessions was the simple use of words and meaningful language.

Since everything in existence has a name – a word to define and describe it, we began playing with words and asked: "Why do we call things what we have always named them?" In other words, (there I go again!), why do we talk about a kitchen, a shovel, a television, a library, a corporation, a doorway, 'habeas corpus' and 'tempus fugit?' Where do the words eyes, ears, nose or mouth, mother, father, children, in-laws and outlaws, etc., etc., etc. have their origin?"

We titled this program: "Watch Your Language!" It proved quite successful. People relaxed, offered suggestions to the questions posed and stress began to subside, as did the angst that usually accompanies it. Participants grew in vocabulary, knowledge and wisdom as well as in their ability to socialize with others. As the classes expanded, we began to develop categories of words, using the basic elements: water, air, earth, fire, as well as plants, animals, trees, mountains seas, birds, fish and the like. Finally, we would ask the participants to begin filling in the lists with their own ideas, according to the specific categories. E.g. (exemplum gratia,), under the category of flowers, they might name lilies, roses, tulips and under that of seas, the Mediterranean, the Caribbean, the Red and others.

The book that you now hold before you came about after many years of reflecting on those people who have and continue to share my life. * It's about the things of creation (all of them) to which I have been introduced, over these past, many years, and the places I have frequented during this exciting journey called life. This book should pique your interest in one or several areas of life in our universe: (or "multi-verse," if you so choose to expand your focus to new horizons.) Some of the topics reflect on the environment of the world handed down to us from over 14 billion years; others are geared to the human response to living in that world, our growth and progress via daily experience, communication and invention. In every instance and, however it all came to be, I give the ultimate glory to God.

You may read this text with the hope of expanding your knowledge, vocabulary or interest in a variety of categories which are found throughout the book. Among these items, you will find birds, fish, animals, games, nursery rhymes, music, sports, various languages rooms of a home, geography and an assortment of food products.

Readers of this book may include teenagers who have a drive for deeper knowledge, middle-age adults and older members of the community. Among this later group one may find elder citizens who attend senior centers, adult day centers or residents of assisted living facilities and the like. Recreation Directors of all types may find the book a workable source for any number of leisure-time activities. As a former senior center director for twenty-five years and currently serving as a chaplain to a wonderful long term care facility and its recreation department, I continually find many opportunities to incorporate the enclosed categories in classes, both formal and not.

Other people of any age will read with the hope of developing 1) their awareness of God's beautiful creation and 2) many examples of how humans co-created with God throughout history. The moon, sun, stars; the sky, land and sea; all of nature in much of its glory speak to the former while various modes of transportation, motion pictures, the arts and many inventions reflect the latter.

Some readers may "wonder" (quite validly, I might add,) why the author did not include several additional lists, e.g., philosophers (Aristotle, Kant, Leibnitz et al.), scientists, psychologists, architects, etc. While there is no limit to the number of categories that could have been included, the point of the text is to encourage you, the reader, to let your mind "wander" as you "wonder" about anything, and everything, in the universe. The final chapters of this book might reflect your very own thoughts and just what you would include should you finally get around to writing your own book.

While individuals can read and study this book within the leisure of their own homes, it may be more profitable for them to participate in a group where people share ideas with one another, thus expanding the multiple examples found within each category. We often limit our vision of God's presence to the sanctuary of a church, a synagogue, a mosque or a temple. This text urges us to look beyond such sacred space to find and give glory to God in all of creation – the first Bible. Theologians and contemplatives join together with Native Americans who see God in everything, naming such, "pan-en-theism," not to be confused with "pantheism" which identifies the essence of God with nature.

Some who have perused sections of this book, before its completion, have suggested that the title, "Watch Your Language," as was the name of the course, mentioned earlier, might be a better fit as the title of this text. However, as was stated above, in the introduction, "everything has a name." So, might we add, does every person and every place, the agreed upon definition of a noun. My thesis, then, is that there is nothing that ever was, or ever will be, which does not fall under the protective umbrella of the One I refer to as God and all are a reflection of that One whom others may see fit to address by another name. A second observation stated that the vast majority of examples, used in each chapter, such as music, radio and television programs, were geared toward an elder population. While this may be true, there is nothing, preventing those of you who are working with children, teens or younger adults, from substituting age-appropriate examples. For a larger portion of the text, anyone who has attained the use of reason, will benefit from the examples provided – and, as anticipated by the author, enlarge upon them.

Based on the Psalms of the Christo-Judaic Scriptures and following the love for God's nature, as evidenced in all of the world's great religions and that of our very own Native American culture, we can proclaim: "All Creation Manifests the Glory of God." (Pss. 18/19 and 148) It is to the God of all creation and to each of you, my friends, that I dedicate this book and I invite you to explore what our God and your neighbors continually share with you.

Peace be with you!
Leo McIlrath

DEDICATION

This book, "All Creation: God's Glory," is dedicated to all of those inspiring people in my life.

Among these, I acknowledge my mom and dad, Florence (Harmon) McIlrath and William A. McIlrath. Brothers, Bill (Milly) and Joe (Hazel) and sisters, Rita (Jack) and Rosemary, as well as Bobby and Theresa, siblings who have been watching from above – years before I was born. To these, I would quickly add my extended family of those early years: Aunt Ruth and Uncle Herb and their children.

As my God called me to priesthood, I was guided by a great number of priests, nuns and lay teachers, each of whom became mentors and who never gave up on me in spite of my learning deficits.

As that same deity, undeterred by man-made rules and traditions, called me to marriage and family, S/He sent me Dianne, already well tested by widowhood – the mother of three loving children, Scott, Jennifer and Brian. And within a short time, our family doubled: Mari, Daniel and Julio – each of these now married to supportive spouses and our grandchildren – have, patiently taught me how to be a better husband, father and grandfather.

But how can I best give credit to each and every person who has, thus far, been an inspiration to me? Allow me to answer that question by offering a simple series of circles, (see accompanying chart) each manifesting people or groups of people who have, in the past, and continue to motivate me – and all for the better. Always centering on Yaweh/God – with family, both physical and spiritual, expanding outward – to relationships established through education, work, athletics, the arts and play, in communal service and prayer – as we age, the list gets bigger and we begin to become aware of the gratitude that each of us owes to so many other companions on our journey of life.

The ministry to which my Father, God, invited me and through which my Brother, Jesus, in His Holy Spirit, anointed me, continues on. I am grateful for those pre-ordained years, in my home town of Danbury CT for very special, lifelong friends; likewise, for the hundreds of seminarians, church members and Duke University Newman Club students, in the diocese of Raleigh, NC; and at this current time, within the residence of the Lutheran Home of Southbury, where I am blessed with the role of Ecumenical and Interfaith Chaplain to an awesome spiritual community. And, finally I dedicate this work to the town people of Sandy Hook/Newtown, their loving children and educators, including each one who is now in heaven, praying for us. The date 12/14 is always in our hearts.

To each of you – I dedicate this simple text – and I challenge you to two tasks: 1) find yourself in this circle and 2) take the time, starting at your early childhood, to make a similar chart – thanking those who have offered you building blocks of a great foundation. You, my friends, as unique parts of God's creation, are likewise, significant to God's glory.

To All of You, I dedicate this book: "All Creation: God's Glory!"

CARES ~ YHWH ~ People in Eucharist ~ Unity in Diversity ~ ...sety

~Family ~Bridgeport Dioc ~ Raleigh~ N.Wilkes ~ Newt. Grove ~

St. Bonaventure U. ~ Christ the King Sem. ~

Clergy - Nuns - Teachers - Classmates - Professors -

Church - Educ - Family - First Friends - Neighbors - Music - Minstrels -

YHWH

Sports - Clubs - Classmates - Havelock~ Duke ~ OBX ~ Weymouth ~ Danbury ES ~ Hosp - St Peter School - DHS - O.L. Mercy Sem. -

Sandy Hook ~ WCSU ~

OUTLINE FOR THE BOOK

Each Chapter follows a similar pattern that should assist the individual (him/her self), parent, group leader, teacher or recreation specialist to guide the participants (ages 7 – 100) to follow this friendly outline prepared for successfully, completing each exercise.

Suggestions for the Leader: Have available

1.) a flip chart or black/whiteboard with dark magic markers (the wider, the better);
2.) hand-out notepads or booklets on which participants might take notes;
3.) make provision for those who have vision or hearing problems, seating them towards the front of the room.
4.) ask each person to speak loudly so that no one is left out of the discussions;

Chapter Outline:

A. A. Introduce the Category to be covered (water-trees-mountains-fish-birds)
o   it is appropriate to quote a writer, famous figure, a book of the Bible, etc.

B. Explain the process – attempt to stay within the category being covered.
o   be aware of the list provided at the start of each chapter but try to refrain from using those words until all have had opportunity to make their own suggestions.

C. Be sure to invite everyone to take part, not allowing a few to hog the activity.
D. When the category appears exhausted (not the participants,) ask if anyone has something else to add to the discussion...
E. Many chapters may have an accompanying list of less familiar terms. You may want to share some of these with them if only to make them aware that there's always room for more in future discussions?

Summary Statements by Leader: Look for feedback on the session. Use this opportunity to set the stage for the next class or session. You may want to give people the title, if at the end of the day, to allow them time to consider the coming topic (s) and look up some words that they may apply at the next class. Ask participants to think of words within the context of a life-setting, e.g., under the topic of water, someone on a cruise; the Exodus journey through the Red Sea; Noah's Ark; swimming at the town park, with friends, as a child.

Applaud participants for their part in the activity and point out how valuable their knowledge is and how beneficial is their willingness to share it with others.

ABOUT THE AUTHOR

Leo McIlrath, born in Danbury, Connecticut, is a graduate of St. Peter Parochial School and Danbury (CT) High School where he participated in a number of athletic programs and several community activities. McIlrath attended Our Lady of Mercy Seminary, in Lenox, MA and St Bonaventure University/ Christ the King Seminary, in Olean NY, where he received a BA Degree in Philosophy and a Masters of Divinity Degree in Theology. As an ordained Catholic Priest, McIlrath served many churches in North Carolina as a pastor, retreat director and as chaplain at Duke University and the US Marine Base at Cherry Point, as well as in several hospitals and nursing facilities.

He resigned from the diocese of Raleigh, in 1976, and pursued a career, working for over 25 years with more elderly constituents, including those in his home-town community Such comprised of the Department of Elderly Services/ City of Danbury, senior centers, adult day centers, and people in long-term care facilities (assisted living communities and nursing homes.) McIlrath served as President for CASCP – The CT Association of Senior Center Personnel and was a state representative to the White House Council on Aging. He is co-founder of the Dorothy Day

House of Hospitality, in Danbury, comprising a soup kitchen and an emergency housing shelter, now in its 33rd year of operation.

McIlrath was awarded a nursing home administrator license from the state of Massachusetts, a Master of Counseling degree from the University of Bridgeport and a DMin (Doctor of Ministry) degree through Global Ministries University. He was a Professor of Latin, Psychology and Gerontology at Western CT State University and taught Gerontology at the University of Bridgeport, while serving as a chaplain to a local hospice agency and supervising health screening for the Western CT Area Agency on Aging.

The author is currently serving as Ecumenical Chaplain at the Lutheran Home of Southbury, in Connecticut, where he celebrates sacred liturgies, offers counseling and leads discussions on a variety of topics, including many of those presented in this text.

In the year of this writing, Pastor McIlrath is celebrating his 50th year of ordination as a Catholic Priest. He lives in Sandy Hook/Newtown, CT with his wife, Dianne. They have six children and eight grandchildren (with more to come – but who's counting?) He can be reached on line through his email address: lionofjudah56@gmail.com

ALL CREATION MANIFESTS THE GLORY OF GOD
May all who read this book find such to be so!

TABLE OF CONTENTS

CHAPTER

*Note: What about the scientists and architects; candle makers and the culinary arts; auto mechanics and newspaper publishers; airline pilots and agricultural geniuses; psychologists and master surgeons? The categories appear unlimited...........so what are we missing? You, the reader, may add it/them here.

_____

_____

_____

_____

_____

_____

ADDENDA

PART I

The God of All Creation

CHAPTER I

The Earth

1.) Basic Elements: (Cf. Addendum XVII)

A) AIR: breathe – spirit – wind – breeze – storm – hurricane – tornado – cyclone

B) EARTH: dirt – sand – clay – mud – stone – rock –ground- trees – woods: forests/jungles – plains – tundra – desert - piedmont – mountains – seashore – earthquakes – tremors

C) WATER: Primeval (above/below the earth Gen 1) –Oceans – Seas – Gulfs- Bays – Straits – Rivers *- Streams – Lakes – Ponds – Aqueducts – Canals – Pools - Ice – Snow – Steam - (Other?)

_____

D) FIRE: Flint – Match – Gun Powder – Dynamite – Lava (Other?)

_____

OTHER RELATED TERMS:

_____
_____
_____

2.) Periodic Table of the Elements: (cf. Chart)

How Many Elements Can You Name?

a) Metals: Iron – Steel – Cobalt – Silver – Zinc – Copper – Tin -

_____
_____

b) Gases: Nitrogen – Helium – Oxygen –

_____
_____

*How do these affect Humans and Other Creatures?

PERIODIC TABLE OF THE ELEMENTS

1																	18
1 H Hydrogen 1.008	2											13	14	15	16	17	**2 He** Helium 4.003
3 Li Lithium 6.941	**4 Be** Beryllium 9.012											**5 B** Boron 10.81	**6 C** Carbon 12.011	**7 N** Nitrogen 14.007	**8 O** Oxygen 15.999	**9 F** Fluorine 18.998	**10 Ne** Neon 20.179
11 Na Sodium 22.990	**12 Mg** Magnesium 24.305	3	4	5	6	7	8	9	..	11	12	**13 Al** Aluminum 26.982	**14 Si** Silicon 28.086	**15 P** Phosphorus 30.974	**16 S** Sulfur 32.06	**17 Cl** Chlorine 35.453	**18 Ar** Argon 39.948
19 K Potassium 39.098	**20 Ca** Calcium 40.08	**21 Sc** Scandium 44.956	**22 Ti** Titanium 47.88	**23 V** Vanadium 50.942	**24 Cr** Chromium 51.996	**25 Mn** Manganese 54.938	**26 Fe** Iron 55.847	**27 Co** Cobalt 58.933	**28 Ni** Nickel 58.693	**29 Cu** Copper 63.546	**30 Zn** Zinc 65.39	**31 Ga** Gallium 69.72	**32 Ge** Germanium 72.61	**33 As** Arsenic 74.922	**34 Se** Selenium 78.96	**35 Br** Bromine 79.904	**36 Kr** Krypton 83.80
37 Rb Rubidium 85.468	**38 Sr** Strontium 87.62	**39 Y** Yttrium 88.906	**40 Zr** Zirconium 91.224	**41 Nb** Niobium 92.906	**42 Mo** Molybdenum 95.94	**43 Tc** Technetium 97.907	**44 Ru** Ruthenium 101.07	**45 Rh** Rhodium 102.906	**46 Pd** Palladium 106.42	**47 Ag** Silver 107.868	**48 Cd** Cadmium 112.411	**49 In** Indium 114.82	**50 Sn** Tin 118.710	**51 Sb** Antimony 121.757	**52 Te** Tellurium 127.60	**53 I** Iodine 126.905	**54 Xe** Xenon 131.29
55 Cs Cesium 132.905	**56 Ba** Barium 137.327	**57 *La** Lanthanum 138.905	**72 Hf** Hafnium 178.49	**73 Ta** Tantalum 180.948	**74 W** Tungsten 183.85	**75 Re** Rhenium 186.207	**76 Os** Osmium 190.2	**77 Ir** Iridium 192.22	**78 Pt** Platinum 195.08	**79 Au** Gold 196.967	**80 Hg** Mercury 200.59	**81 Tl** Thallium 204.383	**82 Pb** Lead 207.2	**83 Bi** Bismuth 208.980	**84 Po** Polonium 208.982	**85 At** Astatine 209.987	**86 Rn** Radon 222.018
87 Fr Francium 223.020	**88 Ra** Radium 226.025	**89 **Ac** Actinium 227.028	**104 Rf** Rutherfordium (261)	**105 Db** Dubnium (262)	**106 Sg** Seaborgium (263)	**107 Bh** Bohrium (262)	**108 Hs** Hassium (265)	**109 Mt** Meitnerium (266)	110	111	112	113	114	115	116	117	118

Lanthanide Series

58 *Ce Cerium 140.12	**59 Pr** Praseodymium 140.908	**60 Nd** Neodymium 144.24	**61 Pm** Promethium 144.913	**62 Sm** Samarium 150.36	**63 Eu** Europium 151.96	**64 Gd** Gadolinium 157.25	**65 Tb** Terbium 158.925	**66 Dy** Dysprosium 162.50	**67 Ho** Holmium 164.930	**68 Er** Erbium 167.26	**69 Tm** Thulium 168.934	**70 Yb** Ytterbium 173.04	**71 Lu** Lutetium 174.967

Actinide Series

90 **Th Thorium 232.038	**91 Pa** Protactinium 231.036	**92 U** Uranium 238.029	**93 Np** Neptunium 237.048	**94 Pu** Plutonium 244.064	**95 Am** Americium 243.061	**96 Cm** Curium 247.070	**97 Bk** Berkelium 247.070	**98 Cf** Californium 251.080	**99 Es** Einsteinium 252.083	**100 Fm** Fermium 257.095	**101 Md** Mendelevium 258.099	**102 No** Nobelium 259.101	**103 Lr** Lawrencium 262

CHAPTER II

Creatures of the Earth

A) Animals – Land:

Elephants – Antelopes – Apes - Armadillos- Bears – Beavers –Tigers – Monkeys - Bobcats-Buffalo –Camels – Caribou - Chinchillas-Chipmunks – Cows – Coyotes - Crocodiles - Deer-Donkey – Panda - Skunk – Wallabies –Weasels – Cats – Horses - Wolves –Yaks – Zebras - Lions – Dogs - Gorillas - snakes

OTHERS?

_____

_____

_____

_____

_____

_____

B) Birds: The Air: **"THE BIRDS OF THE AIR AND THE FISHES OF THE SEA."** (Ps. 8)

Parrots - Condors -Turkeys-Eagles – Owls - Bats –Woodpeckers – Hawks - Pelican - Quail-Geese – Canaries - Chickens- Cicadas- Cockatiels – Cranes - Dodo –Egrets - Cuckoo- Pelicans – Wombats –Storks - Sapsucker - Finches - Robins - Blackbirds - Cardinals -Bluebirds – Seagulls - Pigeons - Crows – Vultures

OTHERS?

_____

_____

_____

_____

_____

C) Fish: The Sea **"AND WHATEVER SWIMS THE PATHS OF THE SEAS."** (Ps. 8)

Salmon- Crab - Shrimp- Angelfish –Seals - Whales-Bass- Dolphins- Sea Lions -Catfish -Crayfish- Tortoise- Lobsters –Starfish – Walruses - Water Dragons -Waterbucks- Zebra fish- Cod – Mackerel - Blue Marlin -Perch -Sword -Tuna -Salmon- Sharks - Blue

OTHERS?

_____

_____

CHAPTER III

Trees, Shrubs and Flowers

A TREES

Elm	Oak
Pine	Maple
Spruce	Holly
Ginko	Loblolly
Magnolia	Hickory
Ash	Redwood
Sequoia	Juniper
Pagoda (Japanese)	Willow
Fir	Pussy Willow
Apple	Pear
Peach	Fig

B SHRUBS

Aloe	Box
Sagebrush	Heather
Dogwood	Laurel
Honeysuckle	Pagoda Bush
Forsythia	Fuchsia
Huckleberry	Loblolly-bay
Ivy	Hibiscus
Hydrangea	Holly
Rose of Sharon Jasmine	
Juniper	Mountain-laurel
Lavender	Honeysuckle

Others?

_____

_____

_____

"CONSIDER THE LILIES OF THE FIELD, HOW THEY GROW; THEY NEITHER TOIL NOR SPIN. YET, I TELL YOU, EVEN SOLOMON IN ALL HIS GLORY WAS NOT ARRAYED LIKE ONE OF THESE." MT. 6

C – FLOWERS: Primrose – Pansies – Jasmine – Jacobs Ladder– Orchid – Peony – Narcissus

Carnation – Chrysanthemum – Anemones – Amaryllis– Iris – Snapdragon – Hyacinths – Aster – Lily

Sunflower – Sweet Pea – Rose –Tulip – Violet– Heather – Hydrangea – Gladiolus – Impatiens

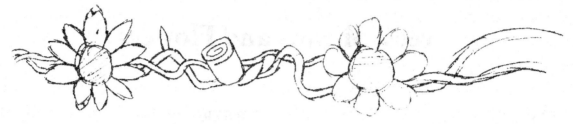

Others?

_____

_____

CHAPTER IV

Ultimate Geologic Phenomena

1) Mountains: Everest, McKinley, Washington -

_____

2) Oceans: Atlantic, Pacific, Indian, Arctic -

_____

3) Seas: Mediterranean, Caribbean, Black -

_____

4) Rivers: Nile, Amazon, Yellow, Rhine, Mississippi, Missouri, Hudson -

_____

5) Lakes: Titicaca, Great Lakes (Huron, Erie, Ontario, Michigan, Superior)-

_____

6) Gulfs: Mexico, Tonkin -

_____

7) Continents: North and South America; Europe, Asia, Africa, Antarctica; Australia*

_____

   Australia = the smallest continent or the largest island in the world

8) Deepest points on the earth: under the ocean -

_____

9) States of the United States: (Hint – Use the alphabet)

_____

_____

_____

_____

* largest; smallest; source of their names –

_____

_____

_____

10) Best known cities: a) in the USA -

_____

_____

b) in the world

_____

_____

_____

CHAPTER V

Outer Space

Sun

Moon

Stars (Supernovas)

Planets

Solar System

Asteroids

Meteors/ Meteorites

Nebula

Cosmos

Universe (Multi-Verse)

Constellations

Comets

Other:

_____

_____

_____

_____

CHAPTER VI

Our World in Color (& Hidden Meanings)

RED/MAUVE/SALMON ANGER – Economically in debt ("in the red")

WHITE/BEIGE PURITY – LIFE – RESURRECTION - RAGE

BLUE/ SKY/ROBIN/CADET/ NAVY/MEDITERANEAN - SAD – SUBDUED (Boys)

GREEN (40 SHADES in Ireland) AMATEUR – NAÏVE - ENVY

YELLOW/ GOLDENROD/ DANDELION COWARDLY – SCARED (Asian)

PINK/ ROSE/ PEACH/APRICOT/ SUCCESSFUL ("in the pink") (Girls)

PURPLE PASSIONATE

VIOLET

BROWN/ TAN / SIENA/ MAHOGONEY/ BURNT B./ APRICOT

BLACK DEATH - Economically OK ("in the black") (Afro-American)

GRAY AGING (The Graying of America)

INDIGO - BLUISH-VIOLET

Have on Hand – A box of Crayola Crayons and/or a sample of many shades of colors from a paint store

A Mnemonic Device: e.g., Colors of the Rainbow: ROY-G-BIV

R – Red O – Orange Y – Yellow G – Green B - Blue I – Indigo V – Violet

Other Colors:

_____

_____

dandelion - orange - green yellow - yellow orange - violet red - yellow green -blue green
scarlet - apricot - red violet - carnation pink -red orange – tan other:

_____

PART II

People as Co-Creators with God

CHAPTER VII

People at Work/Jobs/Employment

How many types of labor/work can you name?

Secretary – Carpenter – Electrician – Doctor – Teacher – Painter – Plumber – Clergyperson – Custodian – Salon/Barber – Tree Services – Real Estate – Veterinarians – Nurses – Nurse Aides –

Sports & Recreation – Stationary – Printing – Counseling – Photographers – Computer Services – Pest Control – Plumbing – Electricians – Lawyer – Lighting – Locksmiths – Sewer Services – Roofing/Siding –Chimneys – Trash Removal – Auto Parts – Mechanics – Watch Repair – Gift Shops – Bookstores – Lawn Improvement – Surveyors – Home Improvement Marble & Granite - Wine and Alcohol – Restaurants – Emergency Medical – Transportation Fitness & Weight Control – Meat Markets

Other:

_____

_____

_____

What type of work did you do?

_____

What would you have liked to do? (Your dream)

_____

_____

Note: Illustrations used with permission by "Creative Forecasting," Colorado Springs, CO 2005

CHAPTER VIII

Meals and Foods for Nutrition & Succulence

a) Meals:

Breakfast (Break-Fast)

Brunch

Lunch

Coffee Break

High Tea

Happy Hour

Supper

Dinner

Dessert

Snacks

Other:_____

b) Foods:

meats

veggies

fruits

desserts

snacks

Other:_____

c) Drinks:

water fruit juice V8 wine beer liquor soda/tonic/pop

floats/frapes/ice cream soda

Other:_____

D) 1. Pick a Fruit: peach, pear, apple, etc. (and make a list)

_____
_____
_____
_____
_____

2. Select a Vegetable and do the same:

_____
_____
_____
_____
_____

3.) Know any herbs? (no! not your uncle)

_____
_____
_____
_____
_____

FOODS FOR THE BODY

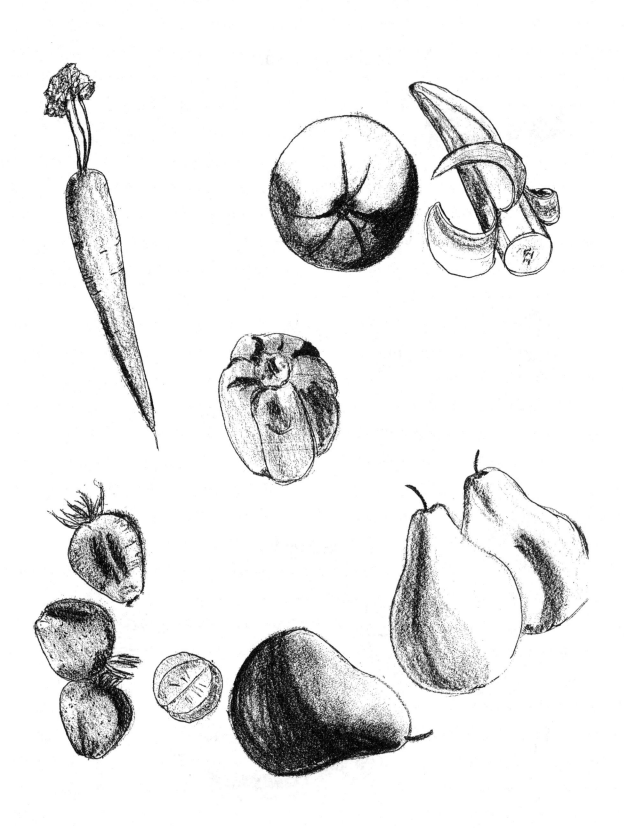

CHAPTER IX

The Human Body and Its Members

A.) EXTERNAL AND VISIBLE:

HEAD

HAIR

FOREHEAD

EYES & EYEBROWS

NOSE

MOUTH/TEETH/ GUMS

CHIN/ BEARD/ MUSTACHE

EARS

NECK

SHOULDERS

ARMS/ BICEPS/ELBOW/WRIST

HANDS/ FINGERS-THUMB/ NAILS

CHEST

STOMACH

WAIST

SEXUAL GLANDS

HIPS

Anus

LEGS/ THIGHS/ KNEES

ANKLES/FEET/ TOES/ HEELS/ NAILS

B.) INTERNAL AND UNSEEN:

BRAIN

ARTERIES, BLOOD

SKIN/TISSUE/SINEWS

NASAL PASSAGES

THROAT/ ESOPHAGAS

BONES/ SKELETAL

INNER EAR/ TYMPANUM

HEART/ LUNGS

STOMACH/LIVER/KIDNEYS

ANAL CANAL

Other

_____

_____

_____

C): THE SENSES: These, Too, Have Limits (What's Your Threshold?)

The following are listed as the "Absolute Threshold" in sensation.

Vision:	candle flame seen 30 miles on a clear dark night
Hearing:	tick of a watch under quiet conditions at 20 feet
Taste:	1 teaspoon of sugar in 2 gallons of water
Touch:	a bee's wing falling on your cheek from ½ in above
Smell:	a drop of perfume diffused into a 3 room apartment *

* Cited in "Introduction To Psychology" a textbook by Dennis Coon, p. 177 (stats are from E. Galanter, "Contemporary Psychphysics" 1962)

CHAPTER X

Emotions (Love Manifested in Many Ways and Words)

A) Filius – (filial) – familiar (family) – "filos-adelphos" Brotherly Love (City of – Philadelphia)

Amicus – (amicable) – friend (ly) – affection – friendship (amicus curiae – friend of the court)

Eros – (erotic) – intimate/ sexual – marital love - passionate

Agape – (Godly Love) – unconditional love for God and neighbor – sacrificial love - (1 Cor. 13)

B) **Poetry and Other Love Stories and Songs**: (share some of yours?)

_____

_____

C) **Terms of Endearment:**

"Lovey" "Darling" "Dearest" Other: _____

"Be My Valentine" (Valentines from our past)

Special Occasions & Events:

"Puppy Love" "Going Steady" Boyfriend/Girlfriend

Engagement (Betrothal) - Courtship

Dowry – contract between fathers of the bride/groom to be

Wedding Ceremonies: (various types: religious or secular)

Marriage – Honeymoon - Anniversaries: Year: 5 – 10 – 25 (Silver) – 50(Golden) – 75(Diamond) - Traditional Gifts)

Children: Biological – Foster Care – Adoption – Step-Children

Other: _____

CHAPTER XI

Personality, Character & Temperament

Happy Sad pleased-contented-upbeat-exhilarated- Beatific Vision - vs. down-depressed-distressed

Popular	-	Unpopular
Gregarious	-	Lonely
Pleasant	-	Angry
Hopeful	-	Despairing
Humble	-	Proud
Excited	-	Dull/ Despondent
Zealous	-	Lazy
Courageous	-	Fearful
Innocent	-	Guilty
Careful	-	Daring/Risky
Thoughtful	-	Selfish
Compassionate	-	Uncaring
Extrovert	-	Introvert
Talkative/Outgoing	-	Quiet

Other?

_____

_____

"HUSBANDS, LOVE YOUR WIVES AS CHRIST LOVED THE CHURCH"
"CHILDREN HONOR YOUR PARENTS" "PARENTS, BE GENTLE WITH
YOUR CHILDREN" "MY BROTHER'S (AND SISTER'S) KEEPER"

CHAPTER XII

Relatively Speaking

Parents: Mom/Dad Children

Siblings: Brother/Sister Kin

Uncle/Aunt Cousins (1st/2nd/3rd...)

Nephew/Niece

Grandfather/Grandmother

Great Grandfather/Great Grandmother

Father/Mother in Law

Son/Daughter in Law

Brother/Sister in Law

Step Father/Mother

Step Son/Daughter

Step Brother/Sister

Consanguinity (Blood Lines)   Affinity (e.g., related through Marriage)

Other:

CHAPTER XIII

Where We Live

1) Towns	2) Streets
Cities	Avenue
Hamlets	Road
Boroughs	Way
Counties	Boulevard
Regions	Drive
States	Highway
Countries	Lane
Nations	
Continents	Interstate
Hemispheres	
Universe	Other:_____

B: Suffixes That Name The Places Where We Live:

-bury (Danbury, Waterbury, Southbury) -burg (Pittsburgh, Plattsburg, Newburg)
`-ville (Pleasantville, Moorsville) -wich (Greenwich, Norwich, Sandwich)
- let (inlet, hamlet) -ton (Clinton, Winston, Wilton)
- ford (Hartford, Milford, Guilford) -boro (Lewisboro, Greensboro, Wilkesboro)
- port (Bridgeport, Williamsport, Newport) -land (England, Scotland, Ireland)

Other: _____

C: Type of Residence: Mobile Home – Trailer - Camper - Motel - Hotel - Time Share

Other:

_____

_____

_____

CHAPTER XIV

A: Rooms in the Home: B: Furnishings

Kitchen: (Cocina It. ; Cuchina Sp)   Refrigerator (Ice Box)

Stove (estuva Sp);   Sink & Counter

Top Table and Chairs   Closets & Drawers (knives, forks, spoons)

Microwave & Toaster   Pantry Windows/Doors (throughout the house)

Other:

_____

_____

Dining Rm: Table & Chairs & Chandelier

Hutch- China Closet

Other:

_____

_____

Living Room (Parlor, Front Room, Sitting Room, Viewing/Receiving Room) Fire Place/Wood Stove

Sofa, Couch, Chairs, Sound System, Radio, Television Lamps, Book Cases

Other:

_____

_____

Bed Room (S) (Master, Guest) Bed (S), Bunks, Pillows, Sheets, Blankets

Dressers, Nightstand, Lamps, Book Case, Mirror, Wall Hangings

Other:

_____

_____

Den: (Man Cave) Desk, Book Cases, Chairs, Filing Cabinets, Sound System

Other:

_____

_____

Bath Room: Sink, Toilet, Tub, Spa, Vanity, Shower Mirrors, Linen Closets

_____

Other:

_____

_____

(Rooms of the House, continued)

Playroom: Pool/Game Table, TV, Dry Bar, Sound System, TV

Other:

_____

_____

Closets: Clothes Racks, Shoe & Hat Spaces

Other:

_____

_____

Basement: (Cellar)   Utilities: Furnace, Electrical Panels, Water Heater

                                   Washer/Dryer, Workbench

                                   Carpets & Rugs (throughout the house?)

Attic: Storage – Spare Bedroom –

Other:

_____

_____

Porches: Front, Back, Side, Decks, Stairs, Veranda:

Other:

_____

_____

CHAPTER XV

That's Entertainment (How We Amuse Ourselves)

HOBBIES

a) The Arts

b) Games (children and adult varieties)

c) Plays, Shows & Musicals

d) Favorite Motion Pictures

e) Stamp/Coins/Baseball Card Collecting

f) First Day Signatures

g) Artifact Collecting: records, postcards, music, paintings, hummels, seashells, etc

h) Reading Books and Magazines; Listening to Tapes, CD's (your favorite to share)

i) Bird Watching

j) Hiking, Walking, Running, Exercise

k) Roller Blading/skating, Ice Skating

l) Table Games: Cards, Chess, Checkers, Ping Pong, Pool, Billiards,

m) Painting and/or Drawing/ Sketching

n) Musical Instruments

o) Horse Shoes, Lawn Bowling, Wiii, Shuffleboard,

p) Pet Care (dogs, cats, ...)

q) Horse riding/ equestrian interests

r)   Target Shooting

s)   Automobiles (restoring, racing, fixing)

t)   Computer (programing, technology)

u)   Writing

v)   Continuing Education Classes

Other:

_____

_____

_____

_____

_____

CHAPTER XVI

Musical Instruments

Keyboards:

Piano (also, Player Piano; Electric Keyboard)

Organ

Harpsicord

Percussion:

Drums (Bass; Snare; Kettle)

Cymbals

Bells; Chimes

Xylophone

Strings:

Violin

Viola

Bass

Fiddle   Guitar   Harp   Banjo

Wind:

Trumpet   Bugle   Saxophone

Tuba   Flute

Other:

_____

_____

CHAPTER XVII

Card Games

Poker

Solitaire

Canasta

Euchre

Blackjack

Rummy

Cribbage

Pinochle

Whist

Go Fish

Old Maid

War

Bridge

Hearts

Crazy Eights

Set Back

Horse

Slap Jack

52 Pick Up

Other:

_____

_____

_____

CHAPTER XVIII

Table Games

Monopoly

Dominoes

Chess

Checkers

Parchesi

Rumi-Kub

Card Games

Go To The Head of the Class

Dice

Bingo

Concentration (Flash Card Memory)

Other:

_____

_____

_____

_____

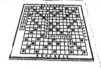

SCRABBLE

SUDOKU

Make every row, column and 3x3 box contain every digit from 1 to 9. (The answer is at the bottom of the page.)

	4				8		7	
3			7					4
	7	9				3	1	
6							9	
			4	7	3			
	8							1
	1	2				4	3	
4				5				6
	9		1				2	

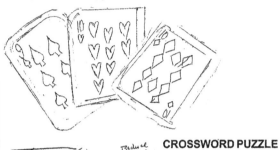

CROSSWORD PUZZLE

Reduce size

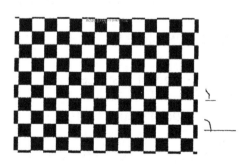

39

CHAPTER XIX

Athletics and Sports

1) Sports Using A Ball:

Baseball & Softball	Football
Basketball	Soccer
Handball	Lacrosse
Racquetball	Kickball
Stickball	T- Ball
Dodge ball	Tennis
Golf	Volleyball
Cricket	Bowling
Polo	Ping Pong
Billiards (Pool)	

2) Track and Field:

Sprints: 100M; 200M; 400M

Distance: 800M; 1600M; 3200M; 5000M; 10,000M

Marathon – Cross Country – Pentathlon; Decathlon

Hurdles: 100M; 400M

Walking: Variety of Distances

Relays: 4 x 100; 4 x 800; 4 x 1600M

Jumps: High J; Long (Broad) J; Pole Vault

Weights: Shot Put; Hammer; Discus; Javelin

3) Grappling: Wrestling; Boxing; Martial Arts; Weightlifting

4) Water Sports: Swimming; Diving; Water Polo; Rafting; Rowing; Surfing

5) Hockey (Field and Ice)

6) Gymnastics: Pummel Horse; Floor Exercise; Balance Beam; Floor Exercises; Parallel & High Bars

7) Other: Hang gliding Parachuting Skateboarding Sky Diving Curling

Hunting: Fishing: Target Shooting: (Pistol; Rifle; Bow & Arrow) Climbing: Mountain; Rock

8) Motor Sports: Stock Cars; Midgets; Motor Cycle; Airplane

9) Equine Sports: Racing; Jumping; Polo

10) Winter Sports: Ice Skating: Sprints & Distances; Tobogganing;

Hockey; Racing; Sledding; Skiing; Ski Jumping: Ski Boarding;

Other?

_____

_____

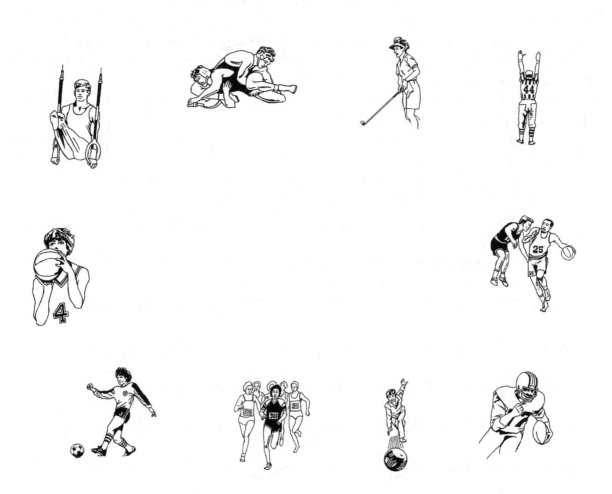

Note: Illustrations used with permission of "Creative Forecasting," Colorado Springs, CT (2005

CHAPTER XX

Schoolyard Games: Old and New

Hide and Go Seek

Tin Can Policeman

Dodge Ball

Marbles

Tag

Snow Goose

May I

May Pole

Simon Says

Ring-a-Round the Rosie

Other:

_____

_____

_____

CHAPTER XXI

Motion Pictures

Ben Hur

King Kong

The Philadelphia Story

Bambi

Snow White and the Seven Dwarfs

From Here To Eternity

Robin Hood

Armageddon

Citizen Kane

Casablanca

Gone With The Wind

Dr. Zhivago

The Godfather

Your Favorite films:

_____

_____

_____

_____

Do You recall when, where and with whom you saw this (these) pictures?

_____

_____

_____

Was there a particular scene or song that remains in your memory?

_____

_____

CHAPTER XXII

Musicals

Fiddler on the Roof

South Pacific

Sound of Music

Joseph and the Amazing Technicolor Dreamcoat

Godspel

Chorus Line

West Side Story

The Wizard of Oz

Other:

_____

_____

_____

_____

Your Favorite Scene or Song?

_____

_____

_____

CHAPTER XXIII

A) Favorite Songs

April Love

See You in September

Mr. Sandman

The Great Pretender

New York, New York

Graduation Song

Other:

_____

_____

_____

_____

B) FAVORITE SONG AND DANCE TEAMS:

Ginger Rogers and Fred Astaire

The Four Aces

The Mariners

Sonny and Cher

The Smothers Brothers

Other:

_____

_____

_____

_____

_____

CHAPTER XXIV

Favorite Hymns

Amazing Grace

A Mighty Fortress

Panis Angelicus

Ave Maria

In The Garden

Holy, Holy, Holy

Alleluia, Alleluia

Sweet Hour of Prayer

Other:

_____

_____

_____

_____

_____

_____

_____

_____

CHAPTER XXV

Comedy Central

A) COMEDIANS

Groucho Marks

Milton Bearle

Bob Hope

Phyllis Diller

Carol Burnette

Other:

_____
_____
_____

(B) Comedy Teams

Burns & Allen

Abbott & Costello

The Marks Brothers

Sid Caesar & Imogene Cocoa

Cheech & Chong

Frick & Frack

Martin & Lewis

The Three Stooges

Rowen and Martin

Olsen & Johnson

Other:

_____
_____

CHAPTER XXVI

Modes of Transportation

Horse (& Buggy)

Stagecoach

Automobile

Truck

Train

Plane

Heliocopter

Boat, Ship, Ferry

Bycycle

Motor Cycle, Motor Bike

Ambulance

Hearse

Other:

_____

_____

_____

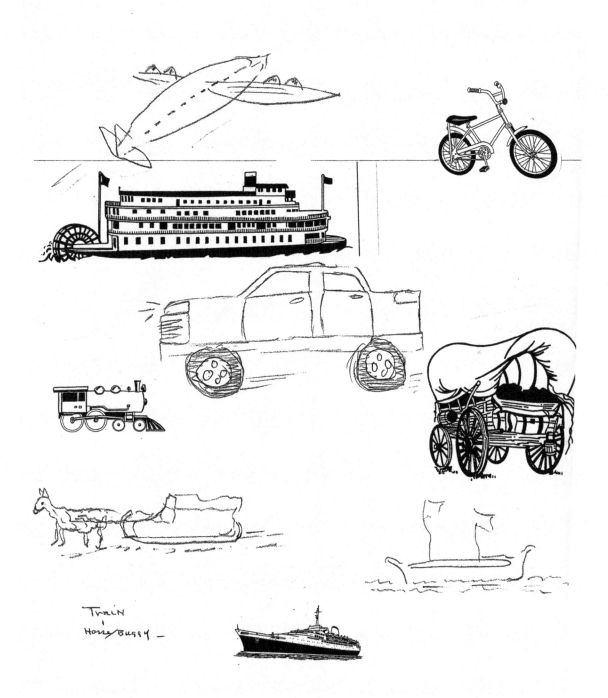

Train
&
Horse Buggy —

CHAPTER XXVII

Means of Communication

A) Conversing with one another

Speaking in vocal sounds

Lip Reading & Sign Language

Smoke Signals & Drums

Telephone: Land, Cell

Telegraph & Walkie Talkie

Radio & Television

Computer.......

B) Hands & Fingers (Signs and symbols)

STOP! GO! COME! CAUTION/ WATCH OUT! THUMB (s) UP/DOWN

+ (PLUS) - (MINUS) x (TIMES) - (Divide) oo (INFINITY)

Universal Signs: Choking (hands to neck) Too Loud/Soft (hands to ears)

Distress: SOS White Flag Ship's Flag upside down

Ask participants for other examples: _____

C. Can You Speak Sign Language

THE Sign Language Alphabet (pictures) – Have a Copy of the basic signs used – for man-woman-hello-farewell-morning evening (demonstrating)

D. Marketting a Business In Other Words:

"Spirits n' Such" "Suds n' Duds" "Close Shave" "Sweet n' Counter" (Be Creative)

Other examples – from where you shop, etc.

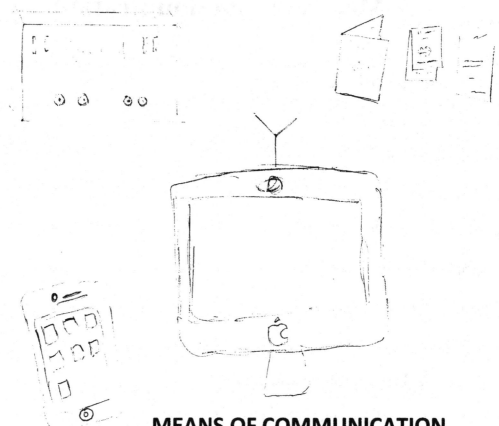

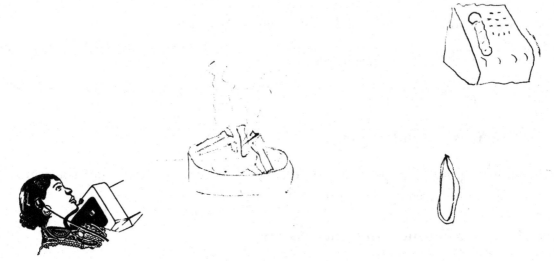

MEANS OF COMMUNICATION

CHAPTER XXVIII

Its About Time

Nanoseconds

Seconds

Minutes

Hours

Days

Weeks

Months

Seasons

Years

Centuries

Millennia

BC/AD & BCE/CE

Eons

Other Terms?

_____

_____

_____

CALENDARS: Old & New: Where the Months Got Their Names (e.g., September = 9th month but its name means 7th. Why? So too Oct=8; Nov=9; Dec=10)......(NOT 10-11-12)

Solar vs. Lunar Calendars: Secular vs. Religious Calendars: Examples?

_____

_____

Many Cultures Have Their Own "New Years Day" (Chinese-Jews-Moslems-Hindus)

Do you know any of these?

_____

_____

_____

TIME PAGE: (Samples of Clocks)

CHAPTER XXIX

Back to Basics in Language

(A) Alphabets in Many Languages (cf. Addendum VIII)

"A-B-C" "Alpha-Beta-Gamma" "Aleph-Bet-Ghimel" "Alif-Bat"

(B) Parts of Speech:	**EXAMPLE:**
NOUN	BOY-GIRL-HOUSE-CITY-DESK-TEACHER
PRONOUN	I-YOU-HE-SHE-IT-WE-YOU-THEY-ME-HIM-HER-THEM
ADJECTIVE	HANDSOME-PREETY-SUNNY-WINDY=BIG-SMALL
VERB	LIVE-RUN-JUMP-BUY-EAT-KNOW-FEEL-THINK
ADVERB	QUICKLY-SLOWLY-KINDLY-EASILLY-
PREPOSITION	OF-FROM-IN-INTO-OUT OF-AWAY FROM-WITH
CONJUNCTION	AND-BUT-OR-NOR-YET
INTERJECTION	WOW!-YEH!-HI!-YIPPEE!-OW!-O MY!

CATEGORIES FOR WORD STRUCTURE:

Verbs:

Person: First – Second- Third Number: Singular (I-You-He/She/It) Plural (We-You-They)

Mood: Indicative – Interrogative – Imperative Voice: Active – Passive

Tense: Present – Past (Imperfect) – Future – Perfect – Past Perfect – Future Perfect

Nouns:

Case: Nominative (Subject) Objective – (Direct Object – Indirect Object – Object of a Preposition)

Predicate Nominative: Noun following "is" or "was" or other forms of "to be"

CHAPTER XXX

Figures of Speech (Cf. Addendum XVI)

LITERAL – the apparent meaning as understood by all

SYNONYMS: the same as: fast – quick late – tardy

ANTONYMS: the opposite: cold – hot

HOMONYMS: bear-beer-bare-bier core-corp- line-lion.

SPOONERISM: "It is kistumary to cuss the bride." (Also Chapter XXXIX)

HYPERBOLE: an exaggerated statement for a heightened effect:
"the whole country turned out for the even

PARABLE: the use of symbols to make one key point (cf. Jesus' Parables

ALLEGORY: seeing multiple symbols in a story

UNDERSTATEMENT: a speaker deliberately makes a situation seem less important than it really is: "Jack Dempsey was a pretty good fighter."

EUPHEMISM: the substitution of an inoffensive term for an offensive one:
"pass away" for died, "collateral damage" for bombing innocent civilians

Also: IRONY - METAPHOR - SIMILE - OXYMORON - PARADOX – PUN

- Can you give an example of some of these?

_____

_____

_____

Other Figures of Speech? (Addendum VII)

_____

_____

_____

Extra: Colorful Language: playing possum – 3 dog night – sly as a fox – eyes like a hawk – swift as a gazelle – soars like an eagle – lazy as sloth – hungry/filthy as a pig – stings like a bee – floats like a butterfly (Muhammad Ali aka Cassius Clay – world champion boxer.)

Add Your Own:

_____

_____

_____

_____

_____

_____

_____

CHAPTER XXXI

Who Knows Any Latin (Or is it all Greek to you?)

<u>A: Simple Derivations</u>: (Word directly into English)

    Labor-Actor-Corpus-Firma-Opus-Mirror-Mobile-Machina

<u>B. Roots of Many English Words</u>:

    Acro-Annus-Aster-Audit-Scriptum-Bio-Biblio-Cornu/Copia

    Digit-Dia-Equi-Terra/Firma-Inter/Intra-Lingua-Manu-Nauta-

    Super/Sub-Magnus/Minus-Tempus/Fugit-Cursus-Ambula

    Con-Contra-Aqua-Unus-Bi-Tri-Quad-Octo-Stella-Pax-Lux

C. <u>Idioms</u>: A. Legal habeas corpus.....ipso facto.......de lege....

        B. Medical per diem....t.i.d. (3 x day) b.i.d. (2x day)

        C. In General: ad infinitum....tempus fugit....terra firma....impedimentum

        (cf list of many idioms: Ch XXXIV)

II. Abbreviations: a.m. p.m. A.D. B.C. C.E. B.C.E I.e. e.g. ibid. N.B.

III. Relationships:

    People: Mater – Pater – Frater – Soror (Sorority) – Filius – Filia – Amicus – (a)

IV. The Body: Corpus Caput – Os – Ocul – Dent – Visio – Audio – Pulmon –

    Digitus (dexterous=right/ sinister=left)– Manus –Collum – Pes - Brachium

V. The House and Home: Domus – Aqua – Gradus – Porta – Ventus – Dormir

VI. Pre-fixes: sub (under)-circum(around)-supra(above)-de(from)-inter(between)

    Intra(within/between)- per(through)-ante(before)-post(after)-anti(against)

CHAPTER XXXII

Much is Greek to Me!

Alpha-Beta-Gamma-Delta-Epsilon-Zeta-Eta-Theta-Iota-Kappa-Lambda-Mu-Nu-Xi-Omicron-Pi-Rho-Sigma-Tau-Upsilon-Phi-Chi-Psi-Omega

1) Body: Cephal (head) – ops/opt (eye) – rhino (nose) –odont (tooth) – stetho (chest) – cardi (heart)- derm (skin) – dactyl (finger/toe) pous/(foot)

2) General Terms: hydro (water)- (tri-three)- therm (heat)- cent (100)- zo (animal)- pachy-derm(thick skin)- hippo-potamus(river-horse)- ana-(back)-chorda(string)- chromo(color)-cursor(runner)- Philos-Sophia(lover of wisdom)

3) Pre-fixes: sub (under)-circum(around)-

   Suffixes: petr-ify(to make into stone)- ana-chron-ism(back-time-state of being)

4) How many Greek words do you recognize from your knowledge of English?

   Dia (across) – angul-gon (angle) Zo (animal) Peri (around) Ana (back)

   Ursa (bear) Mega (big-great-large) Biblio (book) Meta (change)

   Cycl (wheel) Stetho (chest) scope(look at) Polis (city) metropolis Chromo (color)

   Chrono (time) opus (work) Ortho (correct-straight) Meter (measuring device)

   Tele (far-distant) Graph (written record) Ge-gaia (earth)- geography

   Exo (outside-external) Ocul(eye) Ped –pod (foot) Morph (form-shape)

   Giga (large, hugh) mica (glitter-twinkle) glob (globe) sphaira (sphere)

   Eu (good-eustress) cephal (head) cardio (heart) thermo (heat) crypto (hidden, secret) acro (high) eureka!(I have found it!) en (in or on) endo (inside, within)

   Insula (island) mathema (learning-knowledge) Nom/Nomos (law) hydro (water)

   Any Other? (Do you know anyone in a "Soror-ity" or a "Fratern-ity?"

The Christian Scriptures were written in the Greek Language:

CHAPTER XXXIII

Universal Language (Words in Many Languages)

Eng	Lat	Sp	It	Fr	Ger	Gr
Mother	Mater	Madre	Mama	Mere	Mutter	Metera
Father	Pater	Padre	Papa	Pere	Vater	Pater
Brother	Frater	Hermano	Fratello	Frere	Bruder	Adelphos
Sister	Soror	Hermana	Sorell	Jumeau	Schwester	Adelphe
Son	Filius	Filho	Figlio	Fils	Sohn	Teknu
Daughter	Filia	Filha	Figlia	Fille	Tuchter	Kore
Husband	Spousa	Esposo	Marito	Mari/Epoux	Ehemann	Souzugos
Wife	Uxor	Esposa	Moglie	Espose/Feme	Frau	Gunaika
House	Domus	Casa	Casa/Abitazione	Maison	Haus	Ottiti
Light	Lux	Luz	Luce	Lumiere	Licht	Phos
Life	Vita	Vida	Vita	Vie	Leben	Zoe
Love	Amor	Amar	Amore	Amour	Lieben	Agape
Friend	Amigus/a	Amigo/a	Amico	Ami	Freund	Philos
City	Civitatem	Ciudad	Citta	Ville	Stadt	Poli
Man	Homo	Hombre	Uomo	Momme	Mann	Anthropos
Woman	Mulier	Mujer	Donna	Femme	Frau	Gynika
Church	Ecclesia	Iglesia	Chiesa	Eglise	Kirck	Ekklesia
School	Scola	Escuela	Scuola	Ecole	Schule	Scholeio

Can you think of any others?

_____

_____

_____

CHAPTER XXXIV

The Use of Idioms in Everyday Life

"Idiotae et supervacue" (empty headed) e.g., excessive screaming at a ball game)

"Imdedimentum" (excess, both physical and mental baggage that impedes)

"Tempus" fugit" (time flies)

"Bis das; si cito das" (you give twice if you give quickly)

"To err is human; to forgive is divine"

"Fortune is blind"

"Nothing is totally beautiful"

"A remedy for anger is delay"

"Terra Firma" (earth – firm land)

"Quot homines; tot sententiae" (so many people; that many opinions)

"Quod scripsum, scripsit" ("what I have written, it is written:" Pontius Pilate)

"Carpe diem!" (seize the day!)

"Ad infinitum"(forever)

"Cogito ergo sum" ("I think; therefore, I am." Rene Descartes)

"Ex libris" (out of the library of <u>ones name</u>.)

"Mea culpa" (through my fault)

"Esse quam videri" (to be rather than to seem/appear: motto of NC)

Other?

_____

_____

_____

_____

Cf. a book titled: "Amo, Amas, Amat" by Eugene Ehrlich - for a list of multiple idioms from everyday life. Many originate in the Latin Language.

CHAPTER XXXV

Alphabet Soup - The Use of a Acronyms

AA – Alcoholics Anonymous

AAA – American Automobile Association; Area Agencies on Aging

AARP - American Association of Retired Persons

A-O – Alpha – Omega A-B - Alpha Beta (Alphabet) - A-Z (Soup to Nuts)

COA – *Commission on Aging*

ABC Store – *Alcohol Beverage Control*

OSHA – *Occupational Safety Hazards Agency*

HIPPA – *Health Information Portable Privacy Act*

HUD – *Housing & Urban Development*

HEW – *Health Education & Welfare*

CASCP- *CT Association of Senior Center Personnel*

MA – *Municipal Agent*

MO (*What's your?*)

DUI – *Driving Under the Influence* (of drugs, alcohol)

DOA – *Dead on Arrival*

HOMES (The Great Lakes): Huron-Ontario-Michigan-Erie-Superior

RIP – Rest In Peace

Roy-G-Biv (Rainbow colors: Red-Orange-Yellow-Green-Blue-Indigo-Violet)

EGBDF (Music: "Every Good Boy Does Fine") and "FACE"

*IH*S – JES(us) in Greek Letters

Other?

_____

_____

_____

_____

_____

CHAPTER XXXVI

Nursery Rhymes

<u>Hickory Dickory Dock</u>

<u>There Was An Old Woman</u>

<u>Three Blind Mice</u>

<u>Simple Simon Met a Pieman</u>

<u>Humpty Dumpty</u>

<u>London Bridges Falling Down</u>

<u>A Tisket, A Tasket</u>

<u>Pop Goes the Weasel</u>

<u>Mary Had A Little Lamb</u>

<u>Jack Be Nimble, Jack Be Quick</u>

<u>Mary, Mary Quite Contrary</u>

<u>Little Boy Blue</u>

<u>Peter, Peter, Pumpkin Eater</u>

<u>Other:</u>

_____
_____
_____
_____
_____
_____
_____
_____
_____
_____

Illustrations by James Wassmann, grandson of the author. (2015)

CHAPTER XXXVII

The Numbers Game

1. Your Favorite Number: _____ (Why?) _____

2. Popular Numbers:

a) # 1 b)3 (Trinity) c)4 (four leaf clover; 4! golf; "four score and...") d) High 5's e) "come 7, come 11" (dice) 7 churches, angels & seals (in Bk of Rev.) f) ("behind the 8 ball") g) 10's (bowling & yards in football) h) 12 (Tribes of Israel & 12 Apostles) i) 40 (days of rain-Noah's Ark/ 40 years in desert/ 40 days in desert for Jesus and 40 days after Easter – Ascension) j) 50 (days after Passover/Easter - Pentecost);

k) Ages: (the "golden years" 50 the "Golden Age Club"

"55 Alive" -AARP's Driving Course)

60 (– a senior citizen) 62 - 65 (Medicare and Social Security availability)

100 (Centenarian) 100% (giving it all; perfect score on a tes)

Other:

_____

_____

3. Counting in other languages:

Spanish: uno-dos-tres-cuatro-cinco-seis-siete-ocho-nueve-diez

Latin: unus-a-um/duo-ae-o/tres-tria/quatro/quinque/sex/septem/octo/novem/decem

4. How high can you count in English? 1 – 100: 100 – 1,000: 1,000 – 10,000;
     10,000 – 100,000; 100,000 – 1,000,000 (Million) – 1,000,000,000 (Billion);
     1,000,000,000,000 (Trillion) – Our National Debt is $14+ Trillion Dollars

* Multiply 111,111,111 x 111,111,111 (once you do it, you'll never forget!)

5. Population: My Town:_____ Connecticut:_____
United States: _____North America:_____
Other Continents:_____ Earth:_____

65

6. Roman Numerals: I-II-III-IV-V-VI-VII-VIII-IX-X-XX-XXX-XL-L-LX-LXX-LXXX-XC-C
C-CC-CCC-CD-D-DC-DCC-DCCC-CM-M-MM (Mil) 2015 = MMXV

Ages: Baby/Infant Toddler - Youth - Teen - Young Adult - Adult
Middle Age (40) – Senior (60) Octogenarian (80) Centenarian (100)

Other Interesting Uses of Numbers?

_____

_____

_____

_____

_____

_____

CHAPTER XXXVIII

People: God's Greatest Creation

(We Are From....) (Cf. Addendum XIII)

A) North America:

Canada – United States – Mexico

B) South America:

Argentina – Brazil – Chile:

Others?

_____

_____

_____

C) Central America:

Costa Rica – Guatemala Others:

_____

_____

_____

D) Europe:

Austria – Belgium – The Czech Republic:

Others?

_____

_____

_____

_____

E) Asia:

Japan – Philippines – Korea:

Others?

_____

_____

_____

F) Africa:

Libya – Ghana – Congo:

Others?

_____

_____

_____

_____

_____

G) Antarctica: 5,000,000 sq. miles, parts of which are claimed by various countries.

Can you name a few of them?

_____

_____

H) Australia: (considered a continent by some; an island by others):

- What do you think? (Why?)

_____

_____

_____

Where did the original settlers of America ("Native Americans") come from?

• **The Middle East is prominent in today's world: Can you name a few of the countries that make it up? What do you know about any of them?**

_____

_____

Iraq (Meso-potamia = between the rivers) – Iran (Persia) – Israel – Lebanon – Jordan – Syria – (all significant in biblical and secular history)

CHAPTER XXXIX

Major Composer of Music

Wolfgang Amadeus Mozart – Franz Liszt – Johanne Sebastian Bach – Ludwig Van Beethoven – Franz Schubert – Gorge Friedrich Handel – Irving Berlin – Paul Simon – Aaron Copeland Others:

_____

_____

_____

_____

Do you have a favorite composer? _____

Can you name any of his/her works? _____

Do any of his/her works remind you of an event in your life or in world/ American history?

_____

_____

CHAPTER XL

Favorite Authors & Literary Works

Isaac Asimov- Geoffrey Chaucer – Marcus Tullius Cicero - Robert Frost – John Grisham – Ernest Hemingway – Dean Koontz - James Michener – Eugene O'Neil – Ayn Rand – J. D. Salinger – Doctor Seuss – John Updike .– Thornton Wilder - Tennessee Williams – C.S. Lewis

Others:

_____

_____

_____

_____

Where did you first read any of the works of these authors?

_____

_____

What was the work?

_____

_____

Do you have a Favorite Author?

_____

_____

What was your very favorite Book?

_____

Do you favor Fact or Fiction (or a healthy combination of both?)

_____

_____

Do you have an interest in Poetry? _____ Your favorite Poet? _____

Were you ever in a Book Club?

_____

_____

If you were to write a book, what would be your topic?

_____

_____

CHAPTER XLI

Famous Artists & Schools of Art

Vincent Van Gogh – Salvador Dali – Pablo Picasso

How many can you name?

_____
_____
_____

Your Favorite (s):

_____
_____
_____

Schools of Art: Impressionism – Cubism – Surrealism – Pop Art

Other:

_____
_____

Your Favorite:

_____
_____
_____

Where are some of the best known Museums of Art?

_____
_____
_____

Which Museum is nearest to you?

_____
_____

CHAPTER XLII

Famous Athletes in Many Sports

A) **Baseball: Babe Ruth – Lou Gereg – Joe Dimaggio – Yogi Barra -**
Your Favorite(s):

_____

_____

B) **Football: Jim Brown – Fran Tarkenton – Archie Manning**
Your Favorite(s):

_____

_____

C) **Basketball: Bill Russell – Bob Cousy - Michael Jordan**
Your Favorite(s):

_____

_____

D) **Golf: Arnold Palmer – Jack Nicholson – Tiger Woods**
Your Favorite(s):

_____

_____

E) **Tennis: Arthur Ashe – Jimmy Connors - Serena Williams**
Your Favorite(s):

_____

_____

F) **Hockey: Phil Esposito – Bobby Orr – Bobby Hull**
Your Favorite(s):

_____

_____

G) **Soccer: Beckham – Pele – Cristine Lilly – Diego Maradona**
Your Favorite (s):

_____

_____

H) **Swimming: Your Favorite(s): Mark Spitz – Michael Phelps – Krisztina Egerszegi**

_____

_____

I) **Track: (How many can you name?)**
   1) **Running: Jesse Owens – Jim Thorpe – Usain Bolt**

     _____

     _____

   2) **Jumping: Bob Richards – Dwight Stone – Joyner - Kersee**

     _____

     _____

   3) **Throwing: Parry O'Brien – Valerie Adams – T. Majewski**

     _____

     _____

Note: Since Baseball, Football and Basketball are considered the most popular professional sports throughout the USA, an interesting question might be to ask which states and cities claim the most teams?

Addendum IX offers a good picture of such leagues & teams.

e.g.,

<u>**City:**</u> New York City – Los Angeles – Boston – San Francisco – Chicago

<u>**State:**</u> New York – Texas – California – Pennsylvania – Illinois – Minnesota

Your Choice (s):

Baseball:_____; **Football:** _____; **Basketball:** _____

_____   _____   _____

N.B. Teams no longer where they were located when we were younger:

Boston Braves; Brooklyn Dodgers; New York Giants

Others:_____

_____

Note: The Author suggests that all read up on the history of the "Negro League" and the many fine baseball players before Jackie Robinson was allowed entry into Professional Baseball on a national level.

CHAPTER XLIII

Famous Actors on Stage & Screen

John Wayne – Errol Flynn – Betty Davis – Glen Ford -

Your Favorite(s):

_____

_____

Others:

_____

_____

_____

_____

In What Motion Picture(s) did you see these actors?

_____

_____

Did he/she/they receive any acclaim or awards for their performance(s)?

_____

Can you identify with any of their acting traits or skills?

_____

How did their stage lives resemble their real-world lives? Differ?

_____

_____

CHAPTER XLIV

Favorite Radio Programs of Past Days

Life of Riley – Jack Benny – Fiber McGee and Molly – The Answer Man – Tex Ritter –

The Lone Ranger – Henry Aldrich – Jack Armstrong, the All American Boy – The Shadow –

Fireside Theatre – Fireside Chats (w/ FDR)

Other:

_____

_____

_____

_____

_____

Do any of these programs continue to conjure up memories all these years later?

_____

_____

Do you recall where you were when you heard any of these broadcasts (the living room of your home/ a relative or friend's house?)

_____

_____

CHAPTER XLV

Famous News Reporters of the Past: Radio & Television

Gabriel Heater – Edward R. Murrow – John Cameron Swayze – Huntley and Brinkley –

Other:

_____
_____
_____
_____
_____

Did any of these reporters open/close their broadcasts, so often, that it sticks in your memory even today? E.g., "there's good news tonight." "The President has died..." "The war is over...."

_____
_____
_____
_____

CHAPTER XLVI

Favorite Television Programs of the Past

20 Mule Team – The Colgate Comedy Hour – Howdy Doody – Kukla, Fran & Ollie – Ed Sullivan – Superman – The Answer Man – Life of Riley – Jack Benny – Twilight Zone

How many can you name?

_____

_____

_____

Your Favorite (s):

_____

_____

Do any of these remain in your memory today?

_____

_____

Any particular episode(s):

_____

_____

CHAPTER XLVII

Famous Cowboys/Cowgirls

Roy Rogers – Gene Autry – Tom Mix – The Lone Ranger –

Your Favorite:

_____

_____

_____

_____

_____

_____

_____

Was there a particular movie theater where you saw any of these stars?

_____

Did you attend movies with special friends? Are they still your friends?

_____

CHAPTER XLVIII

Your Favorite State (cf. Addendum X)

Where do you live? (City and State)

_____

Where have you lived in the past?

_____

Where do you hope to live one day?

_____

Why?

_____

What States border your State?

_____

How Many States can you name? (Hint: use the alphabet to guide)

Can you name any of the capitals?

_____

_____

_____

_____

The capital of your state?

_____

Do you know the nicknames of any states? _____ your own? ____

_____

_____

_____

_____

_____

_____

_____

_____

CHAPTER XLIX

Your Favorite President(s)

Who was the President when you were born? _____

The Oldest President? _____

The Youngest President? (Elected) _____ (In Office) _____

The Tallest? _____ The Shortest? _____ The Biggest (Heaviest?) _____

President for the longest time? _____How Long?_____

President for the shortest time? _____ How Long?_____

Who was your favorite President? _____ Why?_____
_____

Whom do you wish might have become president but did not? (Why)
_____

How many Presidents a) died while in office? _____

b) were assassinated while in office? _____

Who were they? _____

Who replaced them?
_____
_____

Some comparisons between Presidents' Abraham Lincoln and John F. Kennedy?
_____
_____

From which States did many/most of the Presidents come from?
_____
_____

Name some of the Parties with which the Presidents were affiliated?
_____
_____

CHAPTER L

Important Historic Figures

A) **"People of the Century: Men and Women who Shaped the Last One Hundred Years" (Time/CBS News) (1)**
Pablo Picasso – Albert Einstein – Theodore Roosevelt – Helen Keller Wilbur and Orville Wright – James Joyce – Franklin Delano Roosevelt Igor Stravinsky – Emmeline Parkhurst – Alexander Fleming – John Maynard Keynes – Mother Theresa – Dorothy Day – T.S. Elliot – Ronald Reagan – Charley Chaplin – Edwin Hubble – Eleanor Roosevelt

B) **Video: "Most Influential People of the 20th Century" (2)**
Winston Churchill – Adolf Hitler- Pablo Picasso – Mohandas Ghandi – Martin Luther King, Jr. – John Lennon – Albert Einstein – Sigmund Freud – Henry Ford – Vladimir Ilyich Lenin – Walt Disney -

C) **The Most Important People in the History of the World:**
Jesus – Alexander the Great – Napoleon Bonaparte – Julius Caesar (3)

Do You Agree?

_____

Your Choices:

_____

_____

_____

Notes (1) Time/CBS News; Simon and Schuster, 1999, NY. Many other figures were listed with stories about each one.

(2) Time Magazine: A Video focusing on the life of each individual chosen.

(3) The Most Important People in the History of the World: Anon. Listings

CHAPTER LI

Forms of Currency

Making Sense (Cents?) of Money

Penny .01 cent Nichol .05 cents Dime .10 cent Quarter .25 cents

Half-Dollar .50 cents 1 Dollar 1.00 2 Dollars $2.00 5 Dollars $5.00

10 Dollars $10.00 50 Dollars $50.00 100 Dollars $100.00 Bill

$500 Bill; $1,000 Bill; $5,000 Bill; $10,000 Bill; $50.000 Bill; $100,000 Bill Bank Notes?

Other? _____

What about the value of **"Salt"** as currency? (caused wars....)

Should we return to the **"Gold Standard?"** Why _____

Why Not? _____

What about **Silver** or other precious **Metals or Gems**? _____

Be Creative! What other forms of currency might we try?

_____

_____

_____

Where do the words, **penny – nichol – dime –quarter – dollar** come from? Did you ever see a **"hey penny?"** (Other monetary words?)

CHAPTER LII

A Category of your Choice: What would it Be?

Category (ies?)

1 _____

_____

2 _____

_____

3_____

_____

Given the generic name for your category, what would be some of the specific types of that general theme? E.g., Category: <u>Apples</u> Type: McIntosh or Arkansas Black, etc. **Category:** Automobiles Type: Ford, Chevy, Buick, etc.

_____

_____

_____

_____

_____

ADDENDA

ADDENDUM I

(A): Religions of the World & Their Sacred Writings

JUDAISM: The Jewish Scriptures: Old Testament – Hebrew Canon: 39 Books ;

Greek Canon: (The Septuagint) - 46 Bks (or portions of Bks)

The Law (Torah)....The Prophets.....The Writings......History of Israel

Christianity: The Christian Scriptures: New Testament 28 Bks: 4 Gospels – 14 Epistles – Acts of Apostles – Revelation (Apocalypse.)

Islam: The Koran – The Prophet Mohammad – The 5 Pillars of Islam

Buddhism: Schools: Theravada (Hinayana): Bks only in Pali and Sanskrit – words of The Buddha; Mahayana (Reformers): Bks in Japanese, Chinese, Tibetan, Vietnamese - Words of many Buddha's

Hinduism: Vedas: 4 types – Bramanas – Upanishad – Sutras – Shastras – Puranas – National Epics

Confuscianism: 5 Ching (Classic) Bks – 4 Shu (Disciples) Bks; Also, Zen Buddhism (Meditation)

Bahai: Tablets of Baha' u 'allah

Taoism: (Lao Tzu) – Bk: Tao te Ching – the Chan Sutras – Diamond & Platform Sutras

B: NAMES FOR THE DEITY AMONG THE WORLD RELIGIONS:

Judaism & Christianity: YHWH – Jehovah – Elohim – Adonai – El Shaddai – Abba – Elyon

Christianity: God - The Messiah – The Christ – Holy Spirit;

Islam: Allah - Buddhism: None - Hinduism: Shiva – Lord Krishnu – Arjuna;

Native American: Great Spirit; Secular: Higher Power

C: Founders – Leaders – Charismatic Figures of the World Religions

Judaism, Christianity & Islam: Abraham –

Judaism & Christianity: Isaac – Jacob – Joseph – Moses – Joshua – The Judges – David – Solomon – The Prophets – Ruth – Esther - Judith

Christianity: John the Baptizer – Jesus – The Apostles – The Disciples – Mary Magdellan The 7 Deacons – Early Christian Men and Women

Islam: Mohammed – (Holders of various titles: "Alim" – "Allamaj" – "Caliph" – "Imam")

Buddhism: The Buddha.....Lord Krishna.......Arjuna..........The Dalai Lama

Hinduism: Gandhi – Ramakrishna - Chaitanya ("Sadhus" – "Yogis" – "Gurus")

Confucianism: Confucius..

Taoism: Lao Tze

Bahai: Baha' u 'allah; The Bab

Other: Spiritism...Animism....Primitive Religions....Polytheistic Religions....

D) Afterlife Concepts:

Judaism: a)"Sheol" (the 'deep pit' where one's 'remains' rest with family and friends); b) various concepts of Heaven (esp.in latter Judaism)

Christianity and Islam: "Heaven," "Hell," "Purgatory"*

Hinduism: "Swarga," "Vaikunth," "Kailas Sattya" (transmigration of souls)**

Buddhism: "Reincarnation"** * Roman Catholics

Note: A very interesting book, comparing many concepts of the world religions is **"One God: One Goal", by John Bocuzzi,** Newtown, CT (2014) published by Create Space

The Golden Rule in Many Faith Traditions

*"Do Unto Others as You would have them Do Unto You."**

Christianity: "All things whatsoever ye would that men should do to you, do ye so to them; for this is the law and the prophets." (Matthew 7:1)

Bahai: "Blessed are those who prefer others before themselves." (Tablets of Baha u' allah)

Confucianism: "Do not do to mpothers what you would not like yourself. Then there will be no resentment against you, either in the family or in the state." (Analects 12:2)

Buddhism: "Hurt not others in ways that you yourself would find hurtful." (Udana-Varga 5:1)

Hinduism: "This is the sum of duty; do naught unto others what you would not have them do unto you." (Mahabharata 5,1517)

Islam: "No one of you is a believer until he desires for his brother that which he desires for himself" (Sunnah)

Judaism: "What is hateful to you, do not do to your fellowman. This is the entire Law; all the rest is commentary." (Talmud, Shabbat 3id)

Taoism: "Regard your neighbor's gain as your gain, and your neighbor's loss as your own loss." (Tai Shang Kan Yim P'ien)

Zoroastrianism: "That nature alone is good which refrains from doing another whatsoever is not good for itself." (Dadisten-i-dink 94:5)

*The saying as, most often, cited.

ADDENDUM III

Wise Sayings in the Bible

FAITH WILL MOVE MOUNTAINS

CAN A LEOPARD CHANGE ITS SPOTS?

EAT DRINK AND BE MERRY

FAT OF THE LAND

CHARITY BEGINS AT HOME

CASTING BREAD UPON THE WATER

DON'T CAST YOUR PEARLS BEFORE SWINE

AS YOU SOW SO SHALL YOU REAP

ASHES TO ASHES, DUST TO DUST

BEATING SWORDS INTO PLOUGHSHARES

BORN AGAIN

BY THE SWEAT OF YOUR BROW

A MAN AFTER HIS OWN HEART

AM I MY BROTHER'S KEEPER?

A WOLF IN SHEEP'S CLOTHING

AN EYE FOR AN EYE AND A TOOTH FOR A TOOTH

ALL THINGS MUST PASS

A SOFT ANSWER TURNS AWAY WRATH

A THORN IN THE FLESH

A TWO EDGED SWORD

Other?

_____

_____

_____

ADDENDUM IV

Mainline Christian Communities

Adventist (Seventh Day) - AME (American Methodist Episcopal) - AME Zion

Amish - Assembly of God - Baptist (American, Southern, Free Will)

Episcopal (Anglican) - Church of Christ - Church of God - Congregational (UCC)

Disciples of Christ - Lutheran (Missouri Synod, ELCA: {Evangelical Lutheran Church of America}, Wisconsin Synod,

Mennonites - Nazarene (Church of The) - Orthodox (Greek, Russian, Coptic, Antiochene, ...)- Pentecostal - Presbyterian (Orthodox, North American)

Quaker (Friends) -Roman Catholic: (including Uniate Catholic - Catholic Churches of the East in union with Rome) - Salvation Army - United Methodist

*There are hundreds of churches under the title: "Non-Denominational Christian".

Likewise, one can find Ethnic/ National Churches in most of the above faith communities

ADDENDUM V

Sacred Rites in Various Religious Traditions

Christianity:

Baptism, Holy Eucharist (The Lord's Supper in many denominations)

Confirmation – Anointing of the Sick (a sacred rite in some traditions)

Reconciliation (Penance/ Reconciliation/ Repentance/) – Marriage – Holy Orders (sacred rites in a few traditions) –

* (all seven rites are considered sacraments to Roman Catholics)

Judaism: Prayer - Circumcision – Bar/Bat Mitzvah - Fasting

Islam: Prayer – Fasting – Charity – Pilgrimage - Ablutions

Buddhism: Meditation- Fasting – Chanting Prayer

Hinduism: Prayer - Cleansing in the Sacred River

Bahai: Prayer – Reflection – Missionary Work

Note: 1) Most of the aforementioned faith traditions practice the rites of prayer, fasting, abstaining, communing, in some form, with others.

2) Ecumenism: the policy of interacting with others within one's religious tradition; e.g., Christians of different denominations with one other.

3) Interfaith: Interacting with people of different religious traditions, e.g., as participating in a Community Thanksgiving Day Service.

4) There are a variety of special expressions within each of the aforementioned traditions. (e.g., Orthodox, Reform, Conservative Judaism)

ADDENDUM VI

Holy Days in Various Religious Traditions

<u>Judaism:</u> Rosh Hashanah – Yom Kippur – Purim – Passover – Succocs – Hanukkah – Tabernacles – Sabbath (All Saturdays)

<u>Christianity:</u> Advent – Christmas – Epiphany – Lent – Holy Week – Holy (Maundy) Thursday – Good Friday – Easter – Ascension – Pentecost – Immaculate Conception* – Assumption*(of Mary) – (All Sundays)

<u>Islam:</u> Ramadan – Eid al Fitr – Mawlid al – Nabi (Muhammad's Birthday) Muharam (New Year) – Ashura – Dhu'l-Hijjah - (All Fridays)

<u>Buddhism:</u> Magha Puja – Sangha Day Vesak Puja ("Buddha Day") – Dharma Day –Vassa (Buddhist Lent) – Pavarana Day

<u>Hinduism:</u> Dinali /Deepawali – Dasara/Dussehra – Makara Sankranti – The Birth of Krishna – Maja Shivrati – Ram Navami – Lord Ganesha Birthday

<u>Bahai:</u> Feast of Baja (Splendor)Ridvan – Ascension of Baha'u'llah – Feasts of many qualities: Jamal (Beauty) – Azamat (Grandeur) – Qawl (Speech)

*Note: Roman Catholic and Orthodox Church Feasts

ADDENDUM VII

Secular Holidays in the United States

New Year Day (January 1)

Dr. Martin Luther King, Jr. (January 18)

Easter Sunday (Varies)

Memorial Day (Last Monday in May)

Independence Day (4ᵗʰ of July)

Labor Day (1ˢᵗ Monday of September)

Columbus Day (October 12)

Veterans/Armistice Day (November 11)

Thanksgiving Day (4ᵗʰ Thursday of November)

Christmas Day (December 25)

Other Special Days:

Valentine Day (February 14)

Mothers' Day (2nd Sunday in May)

Father's Day (3rd Sunday in June)

Groundhog Day:

Seasonal Beginnings: Summer – Fall/Autumn – Winter – Spring

Winter Solstice..........Spring Solstice..........Fall Equinox

ADDENDUM VIII

Languages and Alphabets of Many Cultures and Nations

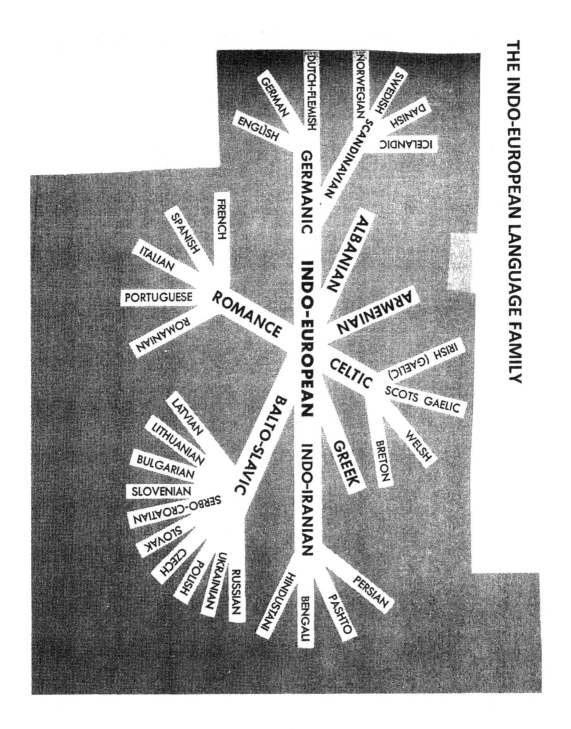

THE INDO-EUROPEAN LANGUAGE FAMILY

COMPARATIVE LANGUAGE CHART OF ALPHABETS

HEBREW	ARABIC	GREEK	RUSSIAN	SANSKRIT	
א aleph – or '	ا alif '	A α alpha a	А а a	अ a	ञ ñ
ב beth b,v	ب bā b	B β beta b	Б б b	आ ā	ट t
ג gimel g	ت tā t	Γ γ gamma g, n	В в v	इ i	ठ ṭh
ד daleth d	ث thā th	Δ δ delta d	Г г g	ई ī	ड ḍ
ה he h	ج jīm j	E ε epsilon e	Д д d	उ u	ढ ḍh
ו vav v, w	ح ḥā ḥ	Z ζ zeta z	Е е e	ऊ ū	ण ṇ
ז zayin z	خ khā kh	H η eta ē	Ж ж zh	ऋ r	त t
ח cheth ḥ	د dāl d	Θ θ theta th	З з z	ॠ r̄	थ th
ט teth ṭ	ذ dhāl dh	I ι iota i	И и Й й i, ĭ	ऌ ḷ	द d
י yod y, j, i	ر rā r	K κ kappa k	К к k	ॡ ḹ	ध dh
כ ך[1] kaph k, kh	ز zāy z	Λ λ lambda l	Л л l	ए e	न n
ל lamed l	س sīn s	M μ mu m	М м m	ऐ ai	प p
מ ם[1] mem m	ش shīn sh	N ν nù n	Н н n	ओ o	फ ph
נ ן[1] nun n	ص ṣād ṣ	Ξ ξ xi x	О о o	औ au	ब b
ס samekh s	ض ḍād ḍ	O o omicron o	П п p	[12] ṁ	भ bh
ע ayin '	ط ṭā ṭ	Π π pi p	Р р r	[13] ḥ	म m
פ ף[1] pe p, f	ظ ẓā ẓ	P ρ rho r, rh	С с s	क k	य y
צ ץ[1] sadi ṣ	ع 'ayn '	Σ σ s sigma s	Т т t	ख kh	र r
ק koph ḳ	غ ghayn gh	T τ tau t	У у u	ग g	ल l
ר resh r	ف fā f	Υ υ upsilon y, u	Ф ф f	घ gh	व v
ש shin sh, š	ق qāf q	Φ φ phi ph	Х х kh	ङ ṅ	श ś
שׂ śin ś	ك kāf k	X χ chi ch	Ц ц ts	च c	ष ṣ
ת tav t	ل lām l	Ψ ψ psi ps	Ч ч ch	छ ch	स s
	م mīm m	Ω ω omega ō	Ш ш sh	ज j	ह h
	ن nūn n		Щ щ shch	झ jh	
	ه hā h		Ъ ъ[9] "		
	و wāw w		Ы ы y		
	ي yā y		Ь ь[10] '		
			Э э e		
			Ю ю yu		
			Я я ya		

ADDENDUM IX

Professional Sports Teams in the United States

A) PROFESSIONAL BASKETBALL TEAMS

AMERICAN LEAGUE

East:

Boston Celtics

Brooklyn Nets

New York Knicks

Philadelphia 76ers

Toronto Raptors

Central:

Chicago Bulls

Cleveland Cavaliers

Detroit Pistons

Indiana Pacers

Milwaukee Bucks

Southeast:

Atlanta Hawks

Charlotte Hornets

Miami Heat

Orlando Magic

Washington Wizards

NATIONAL LEAGUE

Southwest:

Dallas Mavericks

Houston Rockets

Memphis Grizzlies

New Orleans Pelicans

San Antonio Spurs

Northwest:

Denver Nuggets

Minnesota Timberwolves

Oklahoma City Thunder

Portland Trailblazers

Utah Jazz

Pacific:

Golden States Warriors

Los Angeles Clippers

Los Angeles Lakers

Phoenix Suns

Sacramento Kings

Your Favorite Team (s)

_____

_____

Favorite Players?

_____

_____

_____

_____

B) PROFESSIONAL BASEBALL TEAMS

AMERICAN LEAGUE

EASTERN:

    Baltimore Orioles

    Boston Red Sox

    New York Yankees

    Tampa Bay Rays

    Toronto Blue Jays

CENTRAL:

    Chicago White Sox

    Cleveland Indians

    Detroit Tigers

    Kansas City Royals

    Minnesota Twins

WEST:

    Houston Astros

    Los Angeles Angels

    Oakland Athletics

    Seattle Mariners

    Texas Rangers

NATIONAL LEAGUE

EASTERN:

    Atlanta Braves

    Miami Marlins

    New York Mets

    Philadelphia Phillies

    Washington Nationals

CENTRAL:

    Chicago Cubs

    Cincinnati Reds

    Milwaukee Brewers

    Pittsburgh Pirates

    St. Louis Cardinals

WEST:

    Arizona Diamondbacks

    Colorado Rockies

    Los Angeles Dodgers

    San Diego Padres

    San Francisco Giants

Your Favorite Team(s)

_____

_____

Your Favorite Players?

_____

_____

_____

_____

C) Professional Football Teams:

Your Favorite Team (s)

_____

_____

_____

Your Favorite Players?

_____

_____

_____

Note: some team owners are, currently, considering moving their franchises to other locations while retaining the names of their teams, e.g., what happened in the case of the NY Giants who became the San Francisco Giants and the Boston Braves who became first, the Milwaukee Braves, and later, the Atlanta Braves.

ADENDUM X

States/Capitals/Nicknames

STATE	CAPITAL	NICKNAMES
Alabama	Montgomery	Yellow Hammer State
Alaska	Juneau	The Last Frontier
Arizona	Phoenix	The Grand Canyon State
Arkansas	Little Rock	The Natural State
California	Sacramento	The Golden State
Colorado	Denver	The Centennial State
Connecticut	Hartford	The Constitution State
Delaware	Dover	The First State
Florida	Tallahassee	The Sunshine State
Georgia	Atlanta	The Peach State
Hawaii	Honolulu	The Aloha State
Idaho	Boise	The Gem State
Illinois	Springfield	Land of Lincoln
Indiana	Indianapolis	The Hoosier State
Iowa	Des Moines	The Hawkeye State
Kansas	Topeka	The Sun Flower State
Kentucky	Frankfort	The Bluegrass State
Louisiana	Baton Rouge	The Pelican State
Maine	Augusta	The Pine Tree State
Maryland	Annapolis	The Old Line State
Massachusetts	Boston	The Bay State
Michigan	Lansing	The Great Lakes State

Minnesota	Saint Paul	The North Star State
Mississippi	Jackson	The Magnolia State
Missouri	Jefferson City	The Show Me State
Montana	Helena	The Treasure State
Nebraska	Lincoln	The Cornhusker State
Nevada	Carson City	The Silver State
New Hampshire	Portsmouth	The Granite State
New Jersey	Trenton	The Garden State
New Mexico	Santa Fe	The Land of Enchantment
New York	Albany	The Empire State
North Carolina	Raleigh	The Tar Heel State
North Dakota	Bismarck	The Peace Garden State
Ohio	Columbus	The Buckeye State
Oklahoma	Oklahoma City	The Sooner State
Oregon	Salem	The Beaver State
Pennsylvania	Harrisburg	The Keystone State
Rhode Island	Providence	The Ocean State
South Carolina	Columbia	The Palmetto State
South Dakota	Pierre	The Mount Rushmore State
Tennessee	Nashville	The Volunteer State
Texas	Austin	The Lone Star State
Utah	Salt Lake City	The Bee Hive State
Vermont	Montpelier	The Green Mountain State
Virginia	Richmond	The Old Dominion State
Washington	Olympia	The Evergreen State
West Virginia	Charleston	The Mountain State
Wisconsin	Madison	The Badger State
Wyoming	Cheyenne	The Equality/Cowboy State

ADDENDUM XI

The Presidents of the United States

George Washington

John Adams

Thomas Jefferson

James Madison

James Monroe

John Quincy Adams

Benjamin Harrison

John Tyler

James Polk

Zachary Taylor

Millard Fillmore

Franklin Pierce

James Buchanan

Abraham Lincoln

Andrew Johnson

Ulysses S. Grant

Rutherford B. Hayes

James Garfield

Chester Arthur

Grover Cleveland

William Henry Harrison

Grover Cleveland

William McKinley

Theodore Roosevelt

William Howard Taft

Woodrow Wilson

Warren G. Harding

Calvin Coolidge

Herbert Hoover

Franklin D. Roosevelt

Harry S. Truman

Dwight D. Eisenhower

John F. Kennedy

Lyndon Johnson

Richard Nixon

Gerald Ford

Jimmy Carter

Ronald Reagan

George H. Bush

William Clinton

George W. Bush

Barack Obama

Donald Trump

ADDENDUM XII

Famous People Throughout History

Biblical: Adam-Eve-Noah-Abraham-Joseph-Moses-Joshua-David-Solomon-Jesus-Peter-Paul-Matthew-Mark-Luke-John-James-Mary Magdalene-Pontius Pilate-King Herod-Mary, the Mother of Jesus

Non-Biblical: Socrates-Plato-Aristotle-Julius Caesar-Mark Anthony-Cicero-Copernicus-Galileo-Alexander the Great-Genghis Kahn-Eric the Red-Christopher Columbus-Napoleon-Mohammed

Your Choices:

_____

_____

_____

_____

_____

_____

Note: Among the many books, tapes and periodicals published on the topic of famous people, the reader may be interested in the following:

Time/CBS News: "People of the Century: One Hundred Men and Women who shaped the Last One Hundred Years." Simon and Schuster, NY, NY (1999)

A Time/Life Video featuring the "10 Most Influential People of the 20th Century." (Henry Ford – Vladimir Ivan Ilyich/ Karl Marx – Winston Churchill – Adolf Hitler – Pablo Picasso – John Lennon – Mahatma Gandhi – Martin Luther King, Jr. – Albert Einstein – Walt Disney – Sigmund Freud)

ADDENDUM XIII

Countries of the World

COUNTRIES OF AFRICA

Algeria – Angola – Benin – Botswana – Burkina Faso – Burundi

Cameroon – Cape Verde – Central African Republic – Chad – Comoros

Congo – Democratic Republic of The Congo

Cote d'Ivoire – Djibouti – Egypt – Equatorial Guinea

Eritrea – Ethiopia – Gabon – Gambia – Ghana – Guinea

Guinea-Bissau – Ivory Coast (Cote d'Ivoire) – Kenya – Lesotho

Liberia – Libya – Madagascar – Malawi – Mali – Mauritania

Mauritius – Morocco – Mozambique – Namibia – Niger – Nigeria

Rwanda– Sao Tome and Principe – Senegal – Seychelles

Sierra Leone – Somalia – South Africa – Sudan – Swaziland

Tanzania – Togo – Tunisia – Uganda – Zambia – Zimbabwe

COUNTRIES OF LATIN AMERICA

South America

Argentina – Bolivia – Brazil – Chile – Columbia – Ecuador – Guiana (Suriname) – British Guyana – French Guiana – Paraguay – Peru –Uruguay – Venezuela

The Caribbean Islands:
Antiqua and Barbuda – Aruba – Bahamas – Barbados – Cayman Islands – Cuba – Dominica – Dominican Republic – Grenada – Guadeloupe – Haiti – Jamaica – Martinique – Puerto Rico – St. Barthelme Sts. Kitts and Nevis – St. Lucia – St. Vincent and the Grenadines – Trinidad and Tobago – Turks and Caicos Islands – Virgin Islands

Central America

Belize - Costa Rica – El Salvador – Guatemala – Honduras – Nicaragua – Panama

Mexico (*) several geographers consider Mexico and Central America to be a part of North America

Caribbean Islands:

Island Nations of the Caribbean:
Cuba – Haiti – Dominican Republic – Puerto Rico – Jamaica – Trinidad & Tobago – Guadeloupe – Martinique – Bahamas – Barbados – Santa Lucia – Curacao – Aruba – Saint Vincent and the Grenadines – Virgin Islands – Grenada – Antigua and Barbuda – Dominica – Cayman Islands – Saint Kitts & Nevis – Turks & Caicos Islands – Saint Martin – Caribbean Netherlands – Anguilla – Saint Barthelme – Montserrat

COUNTRIES OF EUROPE

Albania Andorra Austria Belarus Belgium Bosnia and Herzegovina

Bulgaria Croatia Cyprus Czech Republic Denmark

Estonia Finland France Germany Greece Hungary

Iceland Ireland Italy

Latvia Liechtenstein Lithuania Luxembourg

Macedonia Malta Moldova Monaco Netherlands

Norway Poland Portugal Romania Russia

San Marino Serbia and Montenegro Slovakia (Slovak Republic) Slovenia Spain Sweden Switzerland

Turkey Ukraine United Kingdom Vatican City

COUNTRIES OF ASIA

Afghanistan Armenia Azerbaijan Bahrain Bangladesh Bhutan Brunei

Burma (Myanmar) Cambodia China Georgia Hong Kong India

Indonesia Iran Iraq Israel Japan Jordan Kazakhstan

Korea, North Korea, South Kuwait Kyrgyzstan

Laos Lebanon Malaysia Maldives Mongolia Myanmar Nepal

Oman Pakistan Philippines Qatar Russia Saudi Arabia Singapore

Sri Lanka Syria Taiwan Tajikistan Thailand Turkey

Turkmenistan United Arab Emirates Uzbekistan Vietnam

Yemen

ADDENDUM XIV

Provinces of Canada

ALBERTA

BRITISH COLUMBIA

MANITOBA

NEWFOUNDLAND

NOVA SCOTIA

ONTARIO

PRINCE EDWARD ISLAND

QUEBEC

SASKETCHEWAN

ADDENDUM XV

States of Mexico

Aguascalientes   Baja California   Baja California Sur   Campache

Chiempas   Chihuahua   Cuahuila de Zaragosa   Culima   Durengo

Guanahuata   Guererro   Hidalgo   Jilasco   Mexico

Michoecam de Ocampo   Morelos   Nayarit   Nuevo Leon

Oaxaca   Puebla   Queretaro de Arteaga   Quintana Roo

San Luis Potosi   Sinaloa   Sonora   Tabasco   Tamaulipas

Tlaxcala   Veracruz   Yucatan   Zucatecas

ADDENDUM XVI

Figures of Speech

SYNONYMS: quick- speedy late – tardy noisy - loud windy-breezy

ANTONYMS: nice – mean tall – short agreeable – disagreeable hot – cold

HOMONYMS: bear-beer-bare-bier core-corp (Diff't spelling/meaning)Same sound)

HOMOGRAPHS: can (tin)-can (able to) (Same spelling/ Diff't meaning) Same sound

EPONYMS: a person (real or mythical) given to a place, period, etc. Wm Penn; Elizabethan

ALLITERATION: the repetition of an initial consonant sound:

"catching cockles with a corkscrew in a creek"

HYPERBOLE: an exaggerated statement for a heightened effect:

"the whole country turned out for the event"

PARABLE: the use of symbols to make one key point (cf. Jesus' Parables)

ALLEGORY: seeing multiple symbols in a story

UNDERSTATEMENT: a speaker deliberately makes a situation seem less important than it really is: "Jack Dempsey was a pretty good fighter."

EUPHEMISM: the substitution of an inoffensive term for an offensive one:

"pass away" for died, "collateral damage" for bombing innocent civilians

IRONY: the use of words to convey the opposite of their literal meaning. The meaning is contradicted by the presentation of the idea. (often humorous or sarcastic.) "the stupid plan was very clever" "the fireboat burned and sank."

METAPHOR: an implied comparison between two unlike things that actually have something in common._"screaming headlines", "all the world's a stage."

SIMILE: comparing two unlike things using "like" or "as."

She has a heart as big as a whale."

OXYMORON: two opposites alongside each other: "giant shrimp"; "sweet sorrow"

PARADOX: a statement inconsistent with common experience:

PUN: a play on words: "Merlin Monroe"; "Atheism is a non-prophet organization."

PERSONIFICATION: a person representing a quality:"the personification of evil"

EPILOGUE

Have you ever had the urge to write a book? I believe that anyone can! When you go to your town's public library, do you wonder just how many books are on those seemingly endless rows of shelving? I have! My home town of 80,000 + residents has a wonderful library of over 100,000 books.

So, why don't you write one of your own? Write one of facts, offering a bit of interesting information about some person, place or thing. Or, if you happen to be a reasonably, good story teller, fiction (or "faction" should it contain some provable facts.) In choosing a subject, you might ask yourself: *"what moves or inspires me? What catches and holds my interest? Music – Sports - The Environment – Careers - Philosophy – Religion - The Weather - Community Action – Gardening – Social Issues - Whatever!"*

Once again, I encourage you, to reflect on, imagine and to begin your book. Start with a word or phrase; then expand it into a sentence and develop your thought into a paragraph, an essay, a story, a finished work. Should you never complete your book, so what? Gaze upon what you have done - and give thanks. You will have used some of your God-given gifts at co-creating and can celebrate your accomplishments.

Leo McIlrath April – 2017 Sandy Hook, CT lionofjudah56@gmail.com

• Please confer the circular chart that lists some of the thousands of people, or groups of people, to whom I extend my gratitude and to whom I dedicate this ongoing work.

ALL CREATION MANIFESTS THE GLORY OF GOD
May all who read this book find such to be so!

LIST OF CREDITS

"All Creation: God's Glory"

Chapter I: Periodic Table of Chemical Elements

Chapter II: Bird illustrations by Alice Carbone from Woodbury, CT, a Volunteer for multiple social and health care agencies and a personal ministerial friend of the author.

Animal illustrations by Ciara Roberson from Hamden, CT, a granddaughter of the author.

Chapter VII: Illustrations on Employment from "Creative Public Forecasting," a Weekly Publication for Activity and Recreation Professionals (2005) Colorado Springs, CO – Editors: Mary Anne Clagett, C.T.R.S., A.C.C. and Pegi Schlis, C.T.R.S., A.C.C.

Chapter IX, Section C – "Absolute Thresholds in Sense Experience," listed in "Introduction to Psychology: Gateway to Mind and Behavior," 10th Ed, (2004) Dennis Coon, PhD, page 177, from a study on Psychophysics - Gallanter

Chapter XVI: Musical Instruments by James Wassmann, grandson of the author, Stratford, CT

Chapter XIX: Illustrations on Athletics from "Creative Public Forecasting," (2005) op sit.

Chapter XXVI: Illustrations by James Wassmann, op sit

Chapter XXXIII: A collage of Alphabets compiled by the author throughout his years of study and teaching.

Chapter XXXIV: for an expanded list of Latin Idioms, the author recommends the book – "Amo, Amas, Amat and More", by Eugene H. Ehrlich, Harper and Row Publishers, Inc. (1985), NYC, NY

Chapter XXXVI: Illustrations by James Wassmann, op sit

Sacred Scriptures used in this text – an assortment of versions, including "The Jerusalem Bible", (1966), Darton, Longman & Todd LTD and Doubleday and Co., Inc., USA; "The Revised Standard Version," Thomas Nelson and Sons, Camden, NJ; "The New American Bible," (1988) Catholic Bible Press, a division of Thomas Nelson Publishers, Nashville, TN

Printed in the United States
By Bookmasters